Help from the air

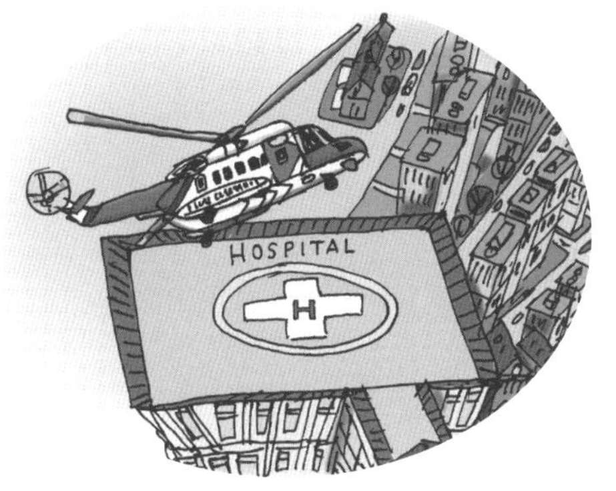

Story written by Liz Miles
Illustrated by Tim Archbold

Speed Sounds

Consonants

Ask your child to say the sounds (not the letter names) clearly and quickly, in and out of order. Make sure he or she does not add 'uh' to the end of the sounds, e.g. 'f' not 'fuh'.

Each box contains one sound. Focus sounds for this story are circled.

f	l	m	n	r	s	v	z	sh	th	ng
ff	ll	mm	nn	rr	ss	ve	zz			nk
ph	le	mb	kn	**wr**	se		se			
			gn		c		s			
					ce					

b	c	d	g	h	j	p	qu	t	w	x	y	ch
bb	k	dd	gg		g	**pp**		tt	**wh**			tch
	ck		gu		ge							
					dge							

Vowels

Ask your child to say the sounds in and out of order.

a	e ea	i	o	u	ay	ee y	igh i	ow o
at	hen	in	on	up	day	see	high	blow

oo	oo	ar	or oor ore	air	ir	ou	oy oi
zoo	look	car	for	fair	whirl	shout	boy

Story Green Words

For each word ask your child to read the separate sounds, e.g. 'b-u-s', 'p-oo-l' and then blend sounds together to make the word, e.g. 'bus', 'pool'. Sometimes one sound is represented by more than one letter, e.g. 'th', 'oo'. These are underlined.

fair-haired snow sense sea

Ask your child to say the syllables and then read the whole word.

lab|ra|dor fan|tas|tic dra|ma|tic har|ness pa|ra|med|ics

ex|tra an|kle moun|tain pro|pell|ers stretch|er

res|cue pi|lot en|gine*

Ask your child to read the root first and then the whole word with the suffix.

trap → trapped tell → telling slow → slowly

attach → attaches lift → lifted freeze → freezing

wrap → wrapped risk → risky flight → flights

** Challenge Words*

Vocabulary Check

Tell your child the meaning of each word in the context of the story.

	definition:	**sentence:**
in despair	*feeling sad and worried*	*They were in despair!*
paramedics	*people who check if you're hurt and look after you on the way to hospital*	*... the others are airlifted into the helicopter where the paramedics can help them.*
risky	*dangerous*	*Airlifts are risky, but you can help people who are trapped or unwell.*
dramatic	*exciting*	*This feels very dramatic!*

Red Words

Red words don't sound like they look. Ask your child to read the words but if he or she gets stuck read the word to your child.

other	two	want	be
could	who	are	people
where	other	could	by
all	one	two	call
small	does	put	were

Help from the air

Do not read the story to your child first. Point to the words as your child reads.
If your child gets stuck on a word help him or her say the sounds and blend them together.
Re-read each sentence to your child to help him or her remember what he or she has read.
Discuss what is happening on each page.

Do you want to be a helicopter pilot?
Do you want to help rescue people?
If so, this is the book for you!

A helicopter pilot can be part of all sorts of rescues. You could be rescuing people from the sea, or maybe people trapped on a mountain.

Let's start with the sea...

Sea rescue

If a ship's engine stops, strong winds can push the ship on to rocks. This is when you get a call telling you that a ship needs help and where it is. You head to the ship as fast as your helicopter can go.

Unless it is very foggy, you will soon spot the ship from the air.

The people on the ship are happy to see you. They were in despair!

The propellers spin to form airflows, so the helicopter can stay as still as possible.

You need to keep the helicopter very steady as the winchman is slowly dropped on to the ship. He attaches a harness on to one of the people and she is lifted up and into the helicopter.

One by one, the others are airlifted into the helicopter where the paramedics can help them.

Mountain rescue

The next day, you are sent to the mountains. You need to rescue two people who are trapped in the snow. One man has tripped and twisted his ankle.

For this rescue, extra help is needed from a rescue dog. This one is a fair-haired labrador called Monty. Dogs have a fantastic sense of smell, so they can sniff for people who are trapped in snow.

Monty soon gets to the man with the twisted ankle and the mountain rescue people follow him.

The man is freezing so he is wrapped in a blanket and put on a stretcher. Then he is lifted on to the helicopter.

My job

Three ways this job is fantastic:

- Airlifts are risky, but you can help people who are trapped or unwell.

- Helicopters can land on and lift off from small bits of land, such as the roof of a hospital. (This feels very dramatic!)

- You can't get bored – it's so good being up in the air.

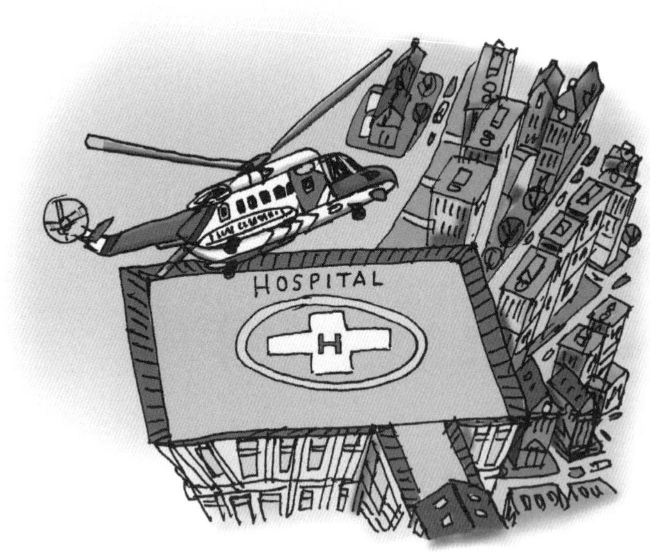

Just one last thing – you will need to have lots of lessons and do lots of practice flights before you can be a helicopter pilot. But I think it is the best job!

Now ask your child to re-read the story helping him or her think about the best way to read each sentence.

Questions to talk about

Read the questions aloud to your child and ask him or her to find the answers on the relevant pages. Do not ask your child to read the questions – the words are harder than he or she can read at the moment.

p.9 Where might helicopter pilots rescue people from?

p.10 Why were the people on the boat in despair?

p.11 Propellers spin to form airflows. What does this help the helicopter to do?

p.12 A man has hurt his ankle in the mountains. Why will he need to be rescued by a helicopter?

p.13 Why is a rescue dog helpful when people are trapped in snow?

p.14 Name one reason why being a helicopter pilot is fantastic.

p.15 Would you like to be a helicopter pilot? Why?

Questions to read and answer

Ask your child to read the questions and find the correct answer in the story.

1. Ships can be pushed on to rocks when it is very **windy / hot / wet**.

2. Helicopter pilots head to the ship as **slowly / quickly / happily** as they can.

3. Pilots need to keep the helicopter **steady / far away / high up** for the winchman.

4. Rescue dogs can sniff for people hidden in the **sea / snow / air**.

5. Airlifts are **boring / simple / risky**.

Speedy Green Words

Ask your child to read the words clearly and quickly – across the rows, down the columns, and in and out of order.

dropped	book	happy	for
start	help	or	spin
air	fast	needs	part
tripped	slowly	bored	stops
sorts	good	three	head